P9-BZU-693

DAT

613.7
LAB

Labrecque, Ellen
Coordination : catch, shoot,
and . . .

$19.99
BC#329121210016674

DATE DUE	BORROWER'S NAME

613.7   BC#329121210016674 $19.99
LAB   Labrecque, Ellen
             Coordination : catch, shoot,
             and . . .

Gunsaulus Academy
Chicago Public Schools
4420 S. Sacramento Ave.
Chicago, IL 60632

Exercise!

COORDINATION

Catch, Shoot, and Throw Better!

Ellen Labrecque

Heinemann
LIBRARY

Chicago, Illinois

Hooray for Exercise!

Exercise gives you energy, stretches your muscles, and keeps your bones strong. It can even improve your thinking skills and help you sleep better.

It is important to exercise every day.

BY THE NUMBERS
Children should watch
no more than one to
two hours of television
a day.

Exercise also provides you with a strong
immune system to fight off colds and the flu.
Let's get moving!

What Is Coordination?

There are five different parts of fitness. They are **stamina**, flexibility, strength, speed, and **coordination**. You need coordination for everything you do. Want to catch a ball? Can you skip or score a soccer goal? All these activities use coordination.

You use coordination skills to get a basketball in a hoop.

The good news is that you can become more and more coordinated in any activity or sport. You just have to practice!

Be Safe

Becoming more **coordinated** doesn't just happen overnight. It takes time and patience to develop skills. When you begin to learn new things, think of safety first. If you want to teach yourself to catch a baseball, use a soft ball that won't hurt if it hits you.

Becoming better at sports is lots of fun—as long as it is done safely.

Always wear a helmet when you ride a bike or skateboard.

A Plus B Equals C!

Coordination comes more naturally if you develop your **agility** and **balance** first. Agility is when you are able to move quickly and easily. Balance is when you are able to keep your body upright and steady while you perform skills.

Standing on one leg is a good way to improve your balance.

If you are agile and can stay balanced, activities such as kicking, throwing, and catching become a lot easier!

 You need to use agility and balance in sports such as tennis.

The Weave

The following game helps with **agility**.
Set up six markers, such as cones, in your backyard. Place three markers in a straight line about three giant steps apart. In between each set of markers, place another marker about three giant steps to the left.

Sprint from one marker to the next, bending down to touch each one with your hand. You will be moving in a zigzag shape and taking small, quick steps.

MINI CHALLENGE BOX
Try doing "the weave" five times in a row, with small breaks in between each session.

You can use tall markers or short markers. Tall markers are easier to reach.

Moving Backward

Backpedaling (running backward) is a great way to develop **agility** and **coordination**. It is tricky to stay **balanced** when your eyes are looking one way and your body is going the other.

On a soft surface such as grass, try backpedaling 50 steps, then **sprint** forward to get back to where you started.

Make sure you have lots of space behind you before you run backward.

People need to use backpedaling in many sports, such as tennis and soccer.

Stork Stand

Balance is important for developing **coordination**. First, try to develop **static** balance, or balance without moving. Pretend to be a stork. Balance on one leg and see how high you can count before you lose your balance.

First, try the stork stand on one leg. Then, try it on the other leg.

2

MINI CHALLENGE BOX

While balancing on one leg, lift up your other leg and touch your foot. See if you can hold this for a count of 10. Switch to the other side.

Which leg are you best at balancing on?

Walk the Line

Find a concrete surface that is smooth and safe to write on with chalk. Draw a straight line with chalk. It should be as long as 10 steps. Walk along the line, placing one foot in front of the other, without "falling off."

Next, try walking backward along the line to get back to the place where you started.

You can use your arms to help you **balance**.

MINI CHALLENGE BOX

Have fun with the chalk. Draw big dots in a pattern, such as a star or rectangle, and try to jump from one dot to the next. Move your feet as fast as you can!

Catching On Your Back

Catching a ball is excellent for **hand-eye coordination**. This is when you are able to make your hands react to what your eyes are seeing. A great catching game is to lie on your back with a tennis ball in your hand. Throw the ball in the air with one hand and try to catch it with the other.

MINI CHALLENGE BOX

See how many times you can throw the ball in the air and catch it without dropping it. Once you reach 15 times, switch hands for the throw and the catch.

Wall Ball

Stand in front of a concrete wall. Make sure the wall has no windows. Throw a tennis ball against the wall with your right hand and catch it with your left hand.

Make sure you throw hard enough to get the ball back into your hand without bouncing.

MINI CHALLENGE BOX

See how many times you can bounce the ball against the wall without dropping it. Once you reach 15 times, switch your throwing and catching hand.

Stay Cool

It is important not to overdo things when you exercise. **Heatstroke** is especially dangerous. This is when the body simply cannot get cool. If you start to feel dizzy or sick, have a headache, or feel muscle **cramps**, it is definitely time for a water break!

If you start to feel sick, you need to stop, rest, and drink water.

For the same reasons, always go slower and take it easy when the temperature outside is especially hot.

 You need to drink more water when you exercise in hot weather.

Eating Well

It is especially important to pick the right things to eat. The healthier you eat, the more energy you will have to exercise and become more **coordinated**. Can you pick the healthier choice for each meal below?

1. Breakfast
A. Sugary cereal with milk
B. Scrambled eggs and whole-wheat toast

2. Lunch
A. Hot dog, bag of chips, and fruit juice
B. Whole-wheat crackers and cheese, apple slices, and yogurt

3. Dinner
A. Pasta, tomato sauce, carrots, and milk
B. Cheeseburger, french fries, and soda

There are lots of tasty foods you can eat that also help your body.

Big Challenge

Tennis is a great sport to play—and it is really fun! It takes **hand-eye coordination** to hit the ball with the racket, especially when you serve and make overhead shots. You could become a strong player with the right amount of practice, positive thinking, and skill. You will be hitting the court before you know it! Game, set, match!

Tennis is a fun sport to play outside in the summer.

Professional tennis players practice for about four hours a day.

Glossary

agility ability to stop and change directions very quickly

balance to hold your body steady

coordination ability to get different parts of the body to work well together

cramps pains you can get when muscles tighten suddenly

hand-eye coordination ability to make your hands react to what your eyes are seeing

heatstroke when the body gets too hot and cannot cool down

immune system parts of your body that help you fight off illness

protein substance in food that gives the body energy and helps it grow. Eggs, meat, nuts, and beans have protein in them.

sprint run very fast for a short distance

stamina power to keep going or keep doing something

static still or fixed position

Find Out More

Books

Schaefer, A. R. *Exercise* (Health and Fitness).
 Chicago: Heinemann Library, 2010.

Senker, Cath. *Healthy Eating* (Healthy Choices).
 New York: PowerKids, 2008.

White, Steven. *Bring Your Raquet: Tennis Basics for Kids.* Minneapolis, Minn.: Kirk House, 2010.

Websites

www.bam.gov
This website is filled with information about fitness and food.

kidshealth.org/kid
This website is devoted to children's health, including exercise, safety, and eating tips.

www.tennis.com
Find out about the world's top tennis players.

Index